Narcissistic Abuse

*How to Recover from Emotional Abuse and
Effects of Narcissism After a Toxic Relationship*

S.TERESA KIDD

Table Of Contents

Introduction

Narcissistic abuse is a real phenomenon. Many people are unaware of how deadly this form of abuse can be in the life of the victim. To a good number of people, abuse does not go beyond the physical and has to do with striking, slapping, or physically harming a person in other forms.

However, the narcissist has more insidious forms of abuse at their disposal and use it to make the lives of their victims, one filled with pain and frustration. The narcissist spends many years slowly destroying those qualities that make their victim unique, until they are under the full control of the narcissist.

Worse still is the fact that when the narcissist gets bored or fails to get the constant supply from the victim, they end the relationship without warning, leaving the victim to pick up the pieces of their life. Some victims can find their way out of this mess and get the healing they deserve, but for others, recovery never happens, and they live with it for the rest of their lives.

The narcissist messes with your memory as the past is hard to forget. After all, you can't pretend it doesn't exist. This is why narcissistic abuse is very damaging. How do you heal from something that you can't forget? How do you recover from an experience that continually keeps popping up in the back of your mind every day? This is where many victims tend to have a problem, and many are unable to get past this phase.

If you have experienced abuse, or you are still experiencing abuse, remember that this is not your fault. You are not responsible for how the narcissist behaves. However, because you are experiencing abuse now or have experienced it at some point in your life does not mean it has to be your story. You can still break free and get the healing you deserve. You do not have to be a victim anymore.

This may seem difficult, but I can assure you that it is possible. I was once a victim of abuse, as I grew up with a narcissistic mother who consistently made me feel worthless and irrelevant. I had a firsthand experience of what it meant for trust to be betrayed by someone who was meant to love you. The great news is that I soon saw my mother for who she was, and that was how my journey recovery began. Over the years, I have picked up various things that worked for me and many others who used to be in the same shoes. I made multiple mistakes along the way, but in the end, I achieved complete recovery and now live the life I desire. The truth is that you can too if you have the right information.

Recovery requires proper information and knowing the right steps to take. However, it is something that requires a reasonable amount of time. This is what makes it essential for you to begin the process as soon as possible. Every minute you waste will only cause more damage to your overall life. You can't just wake up and wish for recovery, as that is only wishful thinking. You need to put in the work and go through all the appropriate steps.

I have included all of the information you will require in this book. And to make it simpler, I have categorized it into chapters to accelerate your reading. They include:

- Chapter 1: This will look closely at narcissists and anarchistic abuse. You will also learn the abuse cycle to help you point it out in your life.
- Chapter 2: This will cover the various types of abuse used by the narcissist to get you under their control
- Chapter 3: Here, you will learn comprehensively about what emotional abuse is and how the narcissist uses it to their advantage.
- Chapter 4: This will expose some of the signs of a narcissist partner to enable you to determine if you are in a relationship with one.
- Chapter 5: In this chapter, you will learn why you are attracting narcissists and some emotional and psychological reasons why you may be refusing to leave the relationship.
- Chapter 6: Will show you all the steps you will need to recover from all of the damage the narcissist in your life may have caused you over the years. You will also learn how to get a new and happy life.

As we noted earlier, narcissistic abuse leaves behind consequences that can stick with you in all areas of your life, to your search for new relationships, new sources of income, and even as you try to make new friends. This means you have to begin the journey to recovery as quickly as possible.

Knowing all of this, let us go together on this journey to help you better understand narcissistic abuse and free yourself from the effects on your life.

Chapter 1: What is Narcissism?

Narcissism is a term that comes from the story of Narcissus in Greek Mythology. He was fated to forever fall in love with the image of himself in a mountain pool. This was his punishment for failing to accept the offer of love made by a young mountain nymph, Echo. Because Narcissus was only able to yearn for but could never have the image that was shown in the pool, he continuously yearned and was ultimately transformed into an appealing flower.

This moral behind this myth is that when excess and obsessive love for one's self expires, only then does genuine lovability and beauty bloom. Narcissists are individuals who are so in love with themselves and have a constant desire to portray the ideal image to other people. Also, they do not have the ability to understand, care, or listen to what others are feeling or saying.

The extreme self-love they have for themselves leaves them with the inability to genuinely and intimately connect with others around them. They are unable to truly let others into their hearts. The ability to let others in is an essential trait as it gives one the chance to experience the difference between the love for others and one's self. This is a core life tutorial and a crucial part of childhood development that these individuals lack.

Narcissists may live their entire lives with a high level of confidence and boastful ego while subtly wishing that they could feel the type of genuine love other typical humans feel. To others, the narcissist may seem like someone who has no empathy or cares for your desires or needs, or as someone who is extremely boastful; this may not be entirely true.

In reality, the narcissist is a person who wishes for a deeper level of emotional connection, which is a requirement that they are unable to understand or accept. Because of all of these needs that the narcissist refuses to accept, or is unable to meet, they tend to have misguided desires. Ultimately, the narcissist is only able to get the attention they require from others through charismatic, appealing, but unsettling habits.

Studies have categorized narcissism as a kind of personality disorder called Narcissistic Personality Disorder. This implies that for one to truly understand what narcissism is, you need to first understand what this disorder is all about.

What is Narcissistic Personality Disorder?

Everyone feels great when they are admired. It can make you feel important and good about yourself. It is also fine to have a great dose of confidence and perhaps be a hype person once in a while. However, when everyone around you starts to attribute you with words such as manipulative, arrogant and controlling, then you may be dealing with Narcissistic Personality Disorder.

This is a disorder that affects about one percent of the population. It is found more often in men than in women. NDP is defined as the lack of capacity to feel empathy for other people, a bloated feeling of self-importance, and an obsessive desire to be admired by other people. Grandiosity is the trademark definition of this disorder, and those experiencing it may be obsessed with vanity, power, and prestige. They may also believe they are better than everyone else and deserve the best treatment and luxuries in life.

It is important to note that a high level of self-esteem and confidence are not the same as NPD. Individuals who have a considerable amount of these attributes still maintain their humility and don't feel they are better than others. People who have NPD have a higher tendency to brag, are selfish, and may ignore the desires and feelings of others.

If you have NPD, there is a chance that it is having a negative impact on your life. This is generally due to experiencing bitterness and anger when people don't give you the special attention and treatment you feel you deserve.

NPD can affect the social, personal, and work relationships of the individual who suffers from an inflated perception of themselves. Often, they are unable to see the damage their unhealthy habits are causing for them and those around them. Many people would prefer not to be around those with NPD, and the sufferers may also deal with a fair amount of unfulfillment in their lives.

Causes of Narcissistic Personality Disorder

Researchers can't pinpoint a specific cause of NPD; however, many agree that it is the result of both environmental and genetic factors. People with NPD have been observed to have a lower amount of gray matter in the anterior insula. This is the region of the brain that has to do with compassion, empathy, and control of emotions.

A number of the characteristics of NPD take place during the typical developmental stages, and scientists believe that this disorder may come to fruition when there is a conflict in these stages.

Some of the kinds of negative environments that interact with the developmental stages include:

- Dealing with severe abuse during childhood
- Learning manipulative tactics from peers or parents
- Having an overly sensitive temperament from the time of birth
- Unreliable parental care
- Being spoiled by peers, parents, and members of the family.
- Having excess praise for positive behaviors and excess criticism for negative behaviors
- Being admired in excess even for undeserved things
- Having too much praise over abilities and looks even when they are undeserved.

It is possible to get a diagnosis from a doctor if you are dealing with NPD. According to studies, a limited number of people ever do this, and if you do go into treatment, it will take time for the treatment to work. However, if you are serious about your well-being and you care for those around you, then it is essential that you seek the proper treatment.

Before an appointment, it's important to write your medical history, experiences, and symptoms. The doctor will then examine the patient, in this instance the NPD sufferer, to ensure there are no other causes for the behavior. Once other possibilities are ruled out, the doctor will recommend a mental health professional.

It's important to follow through with professional treatment if you are serious about ending the cycle of narcissistic abuse. It's also important that you recognize the impact you have on those around you when you engage in this behavior. Surely, you don't want to hurt those you love, or want to love, and you the road to recovery means you will need to be committed to healing... and that means showing for all of your appointments.

What Treatment Options Are Available?

One major technique used in the treatment of this condition is to use psychotherapy. This is also recognized as talk therapy and is utilized to aid the victim in learning how to interact with others around them better. The goal of this is to urge more productive relationships with those around them and to better understand the reason for their feelings.

Treatment for this condition places emphasis on personality traits, and over time, these do not change, and it may take a long time before a breakthrough can be attained using psychotherapy. To change behavior, the psychotherapist will teach the patient how to take responsibility for things they do, and how to deal with other individuals in a non- narcissistic way. Some of these include:

- Dealing with failures and criticisms appropriately
- Controlling and understand feelings
- Accepting and preserving relationships with family and other individuals
- Controlling the need for perfection and unattainable goals.

There are no medications available for the treatment of narcissistic behavior. However, those who experience this condition may also suffer from underlying conditions, such as anxiety and depression. For these conditions, medications can help to manage and even treat them.

In addition, those who live with this disorder have a higher tendency to be dependent on alcohol, drugs or other substances; therefore, it is crucial to treat any addictions for success in treating narcissistic behavior.

It can't be stressed enough that treatment is dependent on participation, and this means showing for all appointments and following all instructions. A narcissistic person can be healed; however, it is paramount to do everything that is advised, when it is advised. Don't think it's something that can be put off for another time. If you're required to do a specific relaxation technique, such as mindfulness, be sure to do so at the instructed time, and don't make excuses.

What Is Narcissistic Abuse?

This is a form of abuse meted out to you by individuals who have the sole goal of taking full control of your life and stopping you from trusting yourself and those close to you. This form of abuse can come from friends, parents, spouses, and even coworkers. Irrespective of the individual who dishes out the abuse, the purpose remains the same; it is to make you lose what makes you unique and take full control of your every being.

The effects of this abuse are enormous and can remain in the life of the victim for a very long time. Besides, the abuse is subtle, and it makes it difficult for others not in the relationship to see that the victim is suffering. It also makes it hard for a victim to ask for help because on the outside, the narcissist seems like the perfect partner.

Narcissistic abuse comes in phases, and we will be looking at all of these phases below.

The Abuse Cycle

The narcissist does not just begin to abuse the victim without due process. There are stages involved in this abuse, and we will review each.

Romanticize

This is the honeymoon phase of the narcissist's relationship with the abuser. The first thing the narcissist does is to let their victim believe they idolize them by using excess flattery and showering them with attention. They put the victim on a pedestal and convince them that they are perfect in every way. Gifts, romantic gestures, loving messages—they are all a part of the game plan.

The narcissist will begin to share the intimate details of their life to build trust. The victim will trust the narcissist and feel they can open up about their life. At this point, the victim lets the narcissist in on their deepest secrets. These secrets will be weaponized by the narcissist later on and used to control the victim.

This excess showering of love shown by the narcissist is categorized as love-bombing. When love-bombing the victim at this stage, the narcissist can learn all the things the victim desires in a partner and behave in the same way. This will give the impression that that the victim has met their soul mate, who is the embodiment of all the victim wants in a partner. However, this is only a façade put on by the narcissist, and it never lasts. And soon, the devaluation phase begins.

Devaluation

One trust is gained, the narcissist will move into the devaluation state. The narcissist will begin to subtly put down the victim in an attempt to make them feel worthless. It begins without warning, and in a way that makes it difficult for the victim to realize they are being tricked. There will be low-key undertones that the victim might not pick up on, such as telling the victim that the yellow shirt they're wearing really isn't their color and perhaps something darker would look better.

The victim doesn't realize that it's just the start of what's to come. After all, it was an innocent opinion, and the narcissist presented it as a suggestion. These 'comments' will increase, and before long, the victim will notice the narcissist runs hot and cold.

During the hot periods, the narcissist might love bomb the victim as they did at the start of the relationship, and then follow with cold periods of shaming and belittling. Because of the manner a narcissist devalues the victim, and it can be very easy to miss. They will insult the victim and cover their tracks by calling it a joke. If the victim tries to complain or call them out on their behavior, they call them irrational or childish. They will resort to name-calling and flirt with other people in the absence of the victim.

To make matters worse, they may subject the victim to the silent treatment when they call them out on their behavior. Also, the narcissist may leverage triangulation techniques, which is when they use someone else to make the victim feel jealous and make themselves appear more appealing. The people they use to triangulate the victim could be the friends of the victim, waiters or waitresses, and sometimes family members. These individuals do not have any boundaries and will be more than willing to use anyone to achieve their goals regardless of who it is. Notwithstanding who they decide to go with, they will make sure the person is emotionally invested in them and they will ensure that the victim finds out about it. They enjoy the thrill of the game and will make the victim feel as if they are competing for their attention and affection.

When the victim calls them out on this unhealthy behavior, they may use projection, deflect, or even call them irrational. They may also leverage the silent treatment for many hours and sometimes months. These toxic individuals will gaslight their victim until they begin to doubt their knowledge, memories, and even feelings. Soon the victim starts to apologize when they did nothing wrong because of the gaslighting.

The narcissist creates an alternate storyline for the victim, which is untrue but suits their own needs. This is what gives them full control of the victim, and the victim will already be doubting their thoughts at this point. The victim will be made to seem like the one who is irrational, bitter and crazy, while the narcissist continues to abuse them in various ways. The narcissist will recreate the entire relationship using their script and allocate all the blame on the victim. With time, the victim starts to develop self-blame and self-destructive behavior, which is what the narcissist wants. For many, it is very traumatic to realize that the person they grew to trust ended up being so different, and that they are, in reality, a chronic abuser.

Discard

The narcissist discards the victim in the most unexpected and painful way possible. This takes place when the narcissist becomes bored with the present victim and wants something new. At this point, the narcissist is done with the victim and will leave abruptly without providing any form of closure to make the blow less painful.

The goal of the narcissist is to make the victim feel insignificant, so they leave them in a way that makes them feel incredibly worthless–like a piece of garbage. Many victims of the narcissist suffer most of their degradation and humiliation during the phases of devaluation and discard. The narcissist does this as a way to prove to themselves that the victim no longer has any relevance to them, even with the amount of abuse they have subjected them to.

Rejection is usually a painful experience, but what the narcissist does is much worse than rejection. Imagine a scenario where a person you have come to love and trust abuses you for a long time, then dumps you unexpectedly and moves on like nothing happened between you. All of the things the narcissist makes the victim experience combined with the unexpected discard is akin to a traumatic event. This is because of the level of frustration and pain it leaves behind in the life of the victim. In the end, it is extremely tedious for the victim to recover fully from all of the effects.

Hoover

This is an extra phase many victims of narcissistic abuse tend to face after the narcissist has discarded them. However, not all victims experience this. There are instances where the narcissist abandons a victim and forgets about them entirely. But in a few cases, the narcissist hangs around the victim and tries to draw them into the life of abuse once more.

In most cases, it happens when the victim initiates the breakup instead of the narcissist. Nonetheless, it is common when the narcissist is unable to get a consistent supply of what the previous victim was offering them, or when a victim is starting to take charge of their life after being discarded.

Many victims are unable to resist and are drawn back into the vicious cycle of abuse, especially if they remain in contact with the narcissist after the relationship. Even if they move on to another relationship, they tend to find a way to wreck it and navigate back to the narcissist.

Narcissists can try to lure their previous victims back at any time. In addition to this, they have no boundaries and can try obstructing the life of the victim without warning, even if they have kids or are happily married. It gives them an ego boost, knowing that they can still get a constant supply from their past victims anytime they want. This way, they can re-enter their lives temporarily, confuse them, and leave once more.

Narcissists may achieve this by text, email, call, or showing up in the home of the victim without warning. They can also do this with the help of a third party, such as a mutual friend. During the process of devaluation, the narcissist temporarily leaves the victim during the relationship. You may believe the victim would be used to it by now, but it is usually worse when the relationship is supposedly over. This is because this works to confuse the victim and make them believe that the narcissist misses them. However, this is not the case, as the narcissist only uses this as a way to get control of the victim once more, especially if the victim was responsible for discarding the narcissist. This way, the abuse can go on, and the narcissist can then discard the victim in the manner they choose.

Why Is Narcissistic Abuse so Deadly?

The abuse cycle conditions the victim to remain apprehensive and cautious throughout the relationship. During the devaluation stage, the victim will do everything possible to resume the romanticizing stage. However, they will only be dragged into another cycle of narcissistic abuse.

Narcissists use the victim's needs for validation, as well as the feeling of irrelevance that they have embedded in the victim throughout the period of abuse, to ensure they remain dependent on them for everything.

The narcissist abuser gives the victim just the right amount of approval, attention, and validation to ensure they do not leave. Instead, they wish they could get back to the time when the narcissist was the wonderful person they had previously met. As the frequency of the abuse increases, the victim tends to develop unhealthy trauma bonds with the narcissist, which can be difficult to eradicate.

In most situations, narcissistic abuse has no time frame and can go on for many years until the victim discards the narcissist. However, it is more common for the narcissist to do the discarding before the victim catches on to their ways.

Victims of narcissistic abuse find it hard to free themselves from the narcissist because of the constant manipulation, projection, and gaslighting. Due to all these, the narcissist urges the victim to believe that they are responsible for the abuse they are experiencing by making them feel they are responsible for the problems in the relationship. Other times, the narcissist manipulates the victim to believe the abuse they are dealing with is not real, and this may result in them toning down the intensity of the abuse.

Many victims who refuse to leave spend most of their time believing and hoping that their abuser will soon change and that they will become the person they first met. Some victims may also be waiting for the next abuse to take place or for the best time to leave the relationship.

A victim needs to understand that when it involves a narcissist, there is no waiting. These toxic individuals never change, and the sooner the victim realizes this and leaves, the sooner they can begin to put their life back together. It is challenging to end a relationship with a narcissist, as we will learn in subsequent chapters; however, healing is more challenging, but with the right information and support, it is something any victim can achieve.

No one deserves to be abused, and if you have ever experienced abuse, don't forget that you are not to blame. Now that you know the basics of Narcissistic abuse, let us head on to the various types of manipulation the narcissist uses on their victims.

Chapter 2: Types of Narcissistic Abuse

For many people, the word abuse usually means that it involves only physical abuse. However, abuse comes in various forms, and the narcissistic individual knows how to leverage them all. Narcissistic abuse may include emotional abuse, physical abuse, financial abuse, and even sexual abuse.

In addition, narcissistic abuse does not only take place in a romantic relationship. It can occur between roommates, family members, and authority figures, and a range of other relationships. All have the same ramifications, and none of them should be undermined. The goal of any form of abuse carried out by the narcissist is to control the victim.

It is essential that one knows the various kinds of abuse the narcissist capitalizes on so you can be sure of what you are dealing with. For this reason, we will be looking into some of the major types of narcissistic abuse below.

Control

This is another type of abuse employed by the narcissist. In fact, this is the goal they have in mind for many of the other forms of abuse the narcissist adopts. Controlling what you wear, who you interact with, when you can leave home, where you can head too, among others, are types of abuse. This can leave a negative impact on the life of the victim.

There are times when the narcissist may also prevent their partner from accessing social media. A narcissist partner will determine when the other partner reads messages, responds to them, and even how they respond by either convincing their partner to allow them access because, after all, they should have nothing to hide, or they will be stealth and watch as they sign in to their social media accounts.

They might check their partner's phone when they are showering or sleeping. If they want to know what their partner is doing every minute of the day and who they are doing it with, which a narcissist will want to know, they will find the means to do so.

Control is not making suggestions or offering helpful advice or being genuinely concerned about the welfare of another, control is using intimidation and manipulation for self-gratification.

A narcissist aims to control every aspect of their partner's life. They use intimidation and threats to gain control. They don't see their victim as a unique individual with their own personality. If a narcissist is unable to get outright control of their victim, they may adopt other forms of abuse to give them this control. One of their top picks is physical abuse.

Physical Abuse

This is the most prominent kind of abuse many people know of. It is what usually comes after emotional abuse, and sometimes they go hand in hand. It involves a situation when the narcissist strikes the victim physically. This form of abuse is not gender or age-based as men, children, and women can all deal with this form of abuse.

Slapping, grabbing them against their will, or touching them in a manner they don't find comfortable can all be termed physical abuse. Some partners may become physical because they had no self-control and were carried away by an argument. However, the narcissist does it in a bid to control the victim.

Regardless of the reason, there is no excuse for physical abuse, and if you are experiencing this in your relationship, it is time to get out. Women are usually at the receiving end of physical abuse, but as we covered earlier, men can be too. If a woman slaps a man, it is also a form of physical abuse and should not be encouraged.

Narcissists believe they have to control their victims by engaging in physical violence, and this can have an impact on the mental well-being of the person too.

Below are a few examples of physical abuse:

- Biting
- Strangling
- Using items in the home as weapons
- Ripping out or pulling hair
- Slapping, scratching, punching, and pushing
- Using weapons to threaten partner
- Subjecting someone to dangerous driving
- Abuse or rough play without consent that results in internal injuries, broken bones, and lacerations.

Physical abuse can be dangerous, and although the goal of the narcissist is to control the victim with it, sometimes it can lead to accidental death. However, it is also intentional in some cases. What this means is that physical violence is a major red flag, and the victim needs to leave the relationship immediately.

Financial Abuse

Here, the narcissist tries to control the finances of the victim, so it is difficult for them to leave the relationship. This form of abuse makes it more difficult for the victim to free themselves from this relationship because they do not have the finances to achieve this. In most cases, the financially abusive narcissist has a good source of income and takes care of the financial needs in the home. Then they prevent their partner from getting a job and handle all of the responsibilities. This is a very typical sign of financial abuse in relationships. If the partner has no job of their own, the narcissist places the cash into an account that the partner has no control over and sometimes no access to. To get cash, they will need the approval and knowledge of the narcissist partner.

Financial abuse can involve income deprivation or withholding income. If a person wants a partner who is wealthy and enters into this kind of relationship without any pressure, then it can't be seen as abuse. However, if with time the person is unable to access funds as they desire, it can be a kind of financial abuse that can ensure the person is unable to leave the relationship when they desire.

There are times when someone who has a good support system may have the capacity to leave the relationship. However, they may be embarrassed or afraid to ask for any form of assistance. In most cases, the victim completely depends on the narcissist for financial support and may not be able to get cash without going through the narcissist. This gives the narcissist full control, and they may withhold cash for clothing, food, and other essential items as a way to punish the victim if they fail to do their bidding.

Below are a few other examples of financial abuse:

- Having bank accounts only in the name of the narcissist
- Control of where, how, and when money is spent
- Forcing partners to sign documents they don't want to, such as taxes and other crucial documents
- Offering an unrealistic allowance
- Refusing to allow the partner to get a job that takes them outside the home

Verbal Abuse

This is another common type of abuse the narcissist leverages. Here, they use their words to cause harm to a person. This could include name-calling or any statement that may cause pain to the victim. There are narcissists who only verbally abuse their partners without laying a finger on them. However, the effect is still the same, and sometimes verbal abuse leaves damage that could last for a long time to come. This is something that should not be present in a healthy relationship.

This type of abuse, similar to others, is something a narcissist uses to gain control. If a victim refuses to do what the narcissist wants, they may resort to verbal abuse until they get what they want.

Another aspect of verbal abuse narcissists love to utilize is shaming. The narcissist partner may spread negative stories about s the victim to cast a bad image in the eyes of others. These stories do not have to be true as long as they achieve the goal of the narcissist.

Violent Threats

This is also another common form of abuse narcissists like to rely on. Here, they use words, motions, gestures, weapons or looks to pass a threat of injury, murder, harm, or fear. In most cases, the narcissist does not have to carry out the threat, but it is still a form of abuse. This is because the goal of this is to get the victim to do something they don't want to do.

Sexual Abuse

Here, the narcissist may sexually harass or assault the victim. Sometimes, they may rape them or forcefully have sex with them without their consent. Being married does not change rape for what it is, and if a partner refuses to have sex at some point, forcing sex is deemed sexual abuse. Many victims are not versed in this form of abuse and keep enduring it in their marriages.

There are many forms of sexual abuse which include:

- Forcing a significant other to strip
- Making a partner take part in sexual activities they are not into
- Forcing a partner to have kids against their will by sabotaging birth control and forcefully having sex with them.
- Forcing a partner to have sex with other people
- Using a sexual name that is very offensive
- Assaulting a partner sexually
- Harming a partner with items while having sex
- Accusing a partner of being promiscuous

When a narcissist tries to use sexual abuse to control their victims, it happens in stages. Their main objective is to make themselves feel superior, live their sexual fantasies even if you are not into them, and dominate you completely. However, not all narcissists use it as a means of control, but many of them do. This is why it is vital for the victim to learn the covert signs of narcissistic sexual abuse so that they can free themselves and get on with their life.

Stages of Sexual Abuse

The Beginning

The first thing a narcissist does is to condition the victim for the abuse. They test the waters to see if the victim will reject their advances or indulge them. They may fondle the victim in inappropriate environments or request sexual favors in the presence of others. These shameful sexual acts aim to make the victim nervous. It is also a way of them to silently let others know that the victim is entirely their property. When the narcissist is called out for their behavior, they will either blame the victim, say they imagined it or they will simply deny.

- **Verbal insults**: Next, is the stage of verbal assaults. This may come as a surprise to the victim because the narcissist was once amazing and knew the right words to say. However, the instant the victim refuses to indulge any of their sexual desires, they may accuse the victim of being controlling. They may also shame the victim for a lack of sexual creativity before increasing the intensity of the insults. They start to use degrading comments about a flaw, which begins to make the victim feel inadequate. The narcissist does not see their significant other as anything other than an item they can have any time they want.
- **Fits of Jealousy**: Soon the narcissist requests the victim to inform them of all their prior sexual encounters and the number of partners they had previously. Sometimes a partner may be curious and not mean any harm by learning this information. But

the narcissist uses this information to justify their bad behavior and may also use it to slut-shame their victim.

Some narcissists may want their victim to dress overtly sexy when heading out, while other times may request they dress less appealing. Regardless of the clothing option, the narcissist will always make the victim feel insecure and accuse them of cheating or trying to attract others. In other cases, the narcissists will use all of these accusations to abuse their victim further sexually, making statements such as, "It is your fault," and "You asked for this." The narcissist can also show jealousy for anything the victim owns that does not allow the attention to stay on them, such as pets, friends or kids.

- **Intimidation Tactics**: To urge the victim to have sex with them, the narcissist may leverage various tactics, including rage, shame, guilt and blame. However, all of these are not sexual abuse to a narcissist, but any forced sex is abusive. For example, the narcissist may urge their victim to have sex with them to validate their feelings or make them feel secure using the victim card.

- **Threats of unfaithfulness**: The narcissist makes threats of cheating with someone else if a victim fails to agree to their many sexual desires. They may also force them to perform sexual activities they don't like and may joke about how attractive their friends are in a bid to isolate their victim. The narcissist will follow through and cheat on the victim to make their point if they don't make any headway with verbal threats.

The Assertive Stage

Regardless of the sexual positions the victim might introduce, and how often they decide to have sex with the narcissist, a narcissist is never satisfied. They won't rest and they'll do all they can to make their victim continuously surpass their limits. Anytime the victim refuses, they scorn them for the position they have chosen and revert to the tricks they used at the start until the victim agrees to their terms. To make the victim see how much control they have over them, they use the refusal as a reason to make the victim pass even more limits.

- **Invoking Fear:** Many victims will concede to the demands of the narcissists out of fear–fear that the narcissist partner may cheat, leave them, hit them, or withhold finances. To make these fears valid, the narcissist will do one or all of them and blame the victim. Then they may request sex as a way to prove the victim had learned their lesson and will do what they want. Regardless of how the narcissist feels at a particular moment, or what their partner's sexual desires are, the narcissist will continue to mount pressure.
- **Insensitive Requests:** As we have stated, sex to the narcissist is only about them and never about their partner. So, they may refuse to use protection while having sex, knowing that they have STD/STIs, and lie

about it. Then when their partner has an infection, they blame you for not being careful enough.

The narcissist views the victim's body as their own, and they feel they have the right to control it. They will say when and where, and control every aspect of lovemaking. They don't care if their partner is satisfied because it's all about the narcissist. The partner is basically a placeholder for sexual release. Often, the sex will be rough and forced, and lacking in any tender intimacy. It is far from the first encounters when the relationship began.

As mentioned, and an important fact that needs frequent reminders, if a victim is forced to engage in sexual contact, it is rape. No victim should allow themselves to be victimized in this manner. If sexual relations are against the will of the victim, don't hesitate to report the incident or incidents to the police. No one has to do anything they don't condone, nor should they. A narcissist will not want to have charges pressed against them as this would negatively impact the exaggerated image they have created for themselves. In any event, a victim needs to get out and get away as soon as feasible.

- **Withdrawing sex**: Some narcissists eradicate sex from their relationship completely. This is a way to keep control of their victim and ensure they do everything the narcissist asks. When the victim tries to find out the reason for stopping sex, the narcissist will point out the lack of sexual creativity, performance and other excuses, and lay the blame on the victim. The narcissist might say the victim is vanilla, and is no longer is exciting.

- **Destroying values**: A narcissist might work hard at destroying any values the victim had when they entered the relationship. They will make unreasonable requests, and if the victim refuses, they will be called a prude or other unflattering names. If the victim agrees to do something that isn't in line with their values, the narcissist will resort to name-calling every time there's a disagreement or a blow-up. The victim will be damned if they do and damned if they don't.

The Violent Phase

Once a narcissist gets to this phase, their goal is to dominate, control, terrorize, or even torture their victim.

This is the wake-up call that the relationship has become too dangerous, and that the victim's welfare is threatened. When a narcissist reaches the violent phase, they have completely lost control of their own sense of self, and they react without thinking of the consequences.

This stage is easy for the victim to recognize, and often those around them have caught on to what's really going on in the relationship.

It's important at this phase that the victim seek help from friends or family or law enforcement. This becomes domestic violence in the worst way, and it is life threatening. At this point, family members or friends need to encourage the victim to leave, and they should make arrangements for their safety.

- **Degrading Activities**: The narcissist may do things to degrade the victim, such as forcing sex or use hurtful objects on genitals. This is often very controlling and the victim is overpowered by the narcissist.

- **Violent Sex**: These acts fall into two categories, mild and critical. Examples of mild, crude sex includes master and slave role-playing, blindfolding, restraints, drugs, and other substances to make the victim immobile.

  Critical cases can cause serious injury or death. Many of you have likely heard of a sexual encounter whereby one of the engaged parties is strangulated to death by a phone cord, rope, or even bare hands. This type of violent sex is dangerous and deadly.

The Exit Phase

When the narcissist abuser is tired of dominating their victim, they may become bored and find another target, leaving the victim with numerous scars to heal from. For some, professional assistance may be required, while others never wholly recover from the abuse. As previously stated, psychological help is just a phone call away.

If you are presently in a relationship as we've been describing, remember that it is not your fault, and you do have the power to get out of the relationship, and you need to leave as soon as possible. You, too, can make an exit before the narcissist decides to leave you. It can be humiliating, so you don't need to let others know your reason for leaving the relationship. Doing so can make your recovery take longer and make you feel more humiliated.

You don't need to tell anyone why you ended the relationship. However, you may need to get help from an experienced therapist to ensure your healing is faster. Still note that, in most instances, exiting from the relationship does not mean it is over. Various things may happen.

- First, the narcissist will move on as if you did not exist and continue with another partner. This can be a frustrating experience for any individual. But this is a norm for narcissists who are not capable of genuine love.
- Second, the narcissist will still have control over you even after the relationship is over. This means they may keep asking you to do sexual acts for them even though you have someone else in your life.

None of these are ideal positions for anyone to be in, and this is why you need to properly heal and recover from abuse before you can move on. We will be covering how you can do this in a later chapter. If you have decided to leave, you need to know that it is fine to feel shock and fear about leaving. There are many ways all of these can influence the remainder of your life, especially if you fail to do anything about it. The image the narcissist creates about you is not real, and you have the power to destroy it.

The main thing you need to understand about all of these is that you are not obligated to have sex with anyone when you don't want to, including your spouse. If your partner forces you even after you explicitly refused, it is abuse and should not be condoned. You are a person with unique needs, and this should be respected. Never forget that.

Chapter 3: Emotional Abuse or Psychological Abuse

This is one of the deadliest forms of abuse the narcissist has in their arsenal. All sorts of abuses are dangerous, but this abuse is subtle and can destroy a person inside. It is a major sign that a relationship is abusive. This form of abuse can be a combination of all the other types of abuse that we have covered, and it is one that can be extremely difficult for a victim to recover from. Many people who experience this kind of abuse never recover from it.

This form of abuse can damage a victim in many ways, as some of them may cut off ties from those they know so they no longer experience this abuse. A victim of this kind of abuse needs to get help as quickly as possible because of how damaging it is.

The reason for this is that it is extremely covert and hard to notice. The damage may have already been done to a victim before they learn of the abuse. The narcissist conditions the victim to believe that abuse is a standard way of life. They soon learn to accept this treatment and view the abuse as something they deserve. The narcissist first earns the trust of the victim before they begin to control and manipulate them. With time, the narcissist moves on to other types of abuse and increases the frequency.

Many victims begin to question their sanity because of how difficult it is to spot the existence of this form of abuse. Many question themselves and think they are crazy. They soon start to disbelieve the things they used to know and their instincts. One of the major ways a narcissist emotionally abuses a victim is by gaslighting, and we will be taking a more detailed look into this concept below.

Gaslighting Technique

Gaslighting is a type of emotional manipulation where a person constantly influences events, which makes the victim start to have doubts about their perspectives and memory. Gaslighting is a subtle form of abuse that results in the victim no longer trusting their instincts. The result of this is their uncertainty about anything.

This form of abuse is one that is loved by narcissists, and it ensures the victim believes every word the narcissist says even if they know the truth themselves. This type of abuse usually comes before other types of physical and emotional abuse. This is because people who have been constantly gaslighted have more probability of staying in the presence of other forms of abuse.

Gaslighting takes place slowly, and the victim does not even know that it's taking place and slowly brainwashing them. It is something that any individual can experience, even those who are seemingly smart.

The Goal of Gaslighting

The core objective of a narcissist who gaslights is to plant doubts in the victim's minds until they disbelieve their memories, thoughts, and feelings. With time, the victim becomes scared of saying what they think because they are worried that they may not accurately portray the events that took place.

There are times when a narcissist gaslighter may create events to ensure they can use these gaslighting techniques. For instance, they may hide something the victim frequently uses, such as their keys, to make them believe they have lost it. Then they help them search for the item they have lost and find it in another location. Continuously doing this may make the victim believe they have a bad memory, and this makes things easier for the gaslighter.

Below are a few common gaslighting techniques a narcissist will employ.

Gaslighting Techniques and Examples

In gaslighting, there is a broad range of techniques available for the narcissist. This is what makes it hard to pinpoint. The narcissist can use these techniques to hide realities that they don't want the victim to know about.

Some of the core gaslighting techniques narcissists may leverage include:

Withholding

The narcissist acts like they do not understand the information the victim is trying to relay. They decide not to listen to the victim and refuse to let their victim in or tell them what they feel.

Some of the statements the narcissist may use here include:

- You are just trying to confuse me.
- Here we go again. I really don't have the energy for your crap today.

Countering

This involves the abuser questioning the victim's memory and explanation of events, even though their version is the right one.

Some statements the narcissists may pick up here include:

- This is how you forgot what happened the last time.
- You said the same thing before, and you were not right!

Using these strategies, the abuser diverts the conversation to something else. This way, the victim starts to have doubts about their perspectives regarding the conversation.

Next, the narcissist starts to question the viewpoints, experiences, and thoughts of the victim using statements like:

- You create too many false stories in your mind.

Diverting or Blocking

At this point, the narcissist starts to question the victim's thoughts and take control of the conversation.

Some of the common examples include

- "Please stop nagging."
- I am not going to do this today again

Trivializing

Here, the narcissist makes the victim believe that all their thoughts and desires are not important. It is also another primary technique in gaslighting, and some examples are:

- You don't care about anyone else. Why must you make every event about you?

Denial or Failure to Recall

This is also another way narcissists gaslight their victims. To do this, they pretend that they don't remember a particular event has occurred. The narcissist may deny making a promise to carry out an activity that is important to the victim.

An example of this is:

- I never promised to do that. You are starting to have illusions again!

The above are some of the major techniques used by narcissists in a bid to gaslight their victim. But there are many other ways they do this. Below, we will be looking into a few of them:

They Isolate Their Victim

It is difficult for the narcissist to manipulate and ultimately control a victim that has a solid support system. This is why they do all they can to eradicate the access the victim has to their support system, which often includes family members, friends and coworkers.

To isolate their victim from their support system, the narcissist may let them in on secrets about them. These may be lies, but the ultimate goal is to destroy the support system.

They may say things such as, "Do your friends like having you around or are they just being nice? I ran into them at the mall today after they told you they canceled a plan for you to go with them." They might also say something, such as, "I saw all your friends at lunch today. Why weren't you there? Weren't you invited?" That plants the seed of doubt in the victim that their friends don't like them around. The narcissist planted this seed in a less transparent way than the first example did, which is more controlling.

Another way to separate the victim from friends is my intercepting calls and messages. Forgetting to tell the victim that a friend called about going to a movie, or telling them that their mother stopped by while they were at work will, of course, result in the victim not responding.

These are just some of the tricks a narcissist will use to plant seeds of doubts in the victim's mind until they destroy the friendship and support system. When the narcissist achieves this, they will become the only person the has to turn to. This way, they can condition their victim into their ideal person and control them as they please.

They Tell Obvious Lies

The narcissist makes a statement to the victim, and even when the victim is certain that it is a lie, the narcissist denies it without batting an eyelid. They do this as a means of preparing the stage so that the victim remains unsure and unsteady. Soon the victim will start to doubt their perception of things by thinking, "Maybe I was wrong about it?"

This goes on until the victim does not trust their instincts anymore, and instead believes whatever the narcissist says. In the end, they take full control of the perceptions of the victim and only tell them what they need them to believe.

Their Words and Actions Don't Match

Jake always told his wife, Rosie, how much she meant to him and the depth of his love for her. However, these were empty promises, and he was always quick to unleash his anger whenever she failed to do something he asked. He always mentioned how unlovable she was and how he was going to soon leave her. Sometimes, he physically abused her, and the next day, he reminded her of how much he loved her once more, leaving Rossie confused as to what was happening.

This is a common way the narcissist gaslights their victim. They say one thing and act completely differently. Their behavior and their statements never align, and this works to keep the victim confused at all times.

They Use Something the Victim Cherishes

Narcissists use something their victim's loves as a weapon. This could be some specific behavior or a part of their identity. The narcissist understands the weakness of their victim and attacks them with this information. They can make them believe that they would only be lovable if they had some characteristics, or behaved in a specific manner. The goal of this is to destroy the victim from the core of their being.

They Project

When narcissists have a quality they don't like, they project it to their victim as a means of manipulation. Regardless if it is their lack of talent, or their inability to tell the truth, or perhaps they are cheating on their partner, they will constantly accuse their victim of the things they are doing in the shadows.

This is a way to distract the victim and make them focus on themselves as opposed to the narcissist.

They Use Positive Reinforcement to Obscure the Minds Of Victims

Paul constantly treated his wife, Martha, with disdain. He never failed to make her understand how irrelevant she was and was quick to point out her flaws at every opportunity. However, sometimes, he let her know how amazing she was when she completed an action. He'd tell her she is a good mother and a skilled cook. Ultimately, this worked at keeping Martha confused.

This is an example of how a narcissist uses positive reinforcement to blur the mind of their victim. When a person who constantly brings you down now gives you praise for something you deserve, it can be extremely confusing. Narcissists who are skilled at manipulation understand this and leverage it. This helps them to ensure their victim does not trust their own perception of things, and instead, trust the perception offered to them by the narcissist.

Crazy-Making

The narcissist understands that if people believe their victim is crazy, is will be impossible for anybody to believe them even when they speak up. This way, the narcissist stays in control and will do anything they want to the victim without fear of repercussion.

In addition to making others believe the victim is crazy, the narcissist also makes the victim believe they are crazy, too. This usually comes after they have managed to isolate them from their support system and have convinced the victim that they are the only reliable ones. The victim starts to see the narcissist as the only person they can trust, and the moment they have started to doubt themselves, their mental health starts to suffer.

Ultimately, the narcissist wants a person who does all they want them to do without question. This is achievable once the victim no longer has any trust in themselves, and soon, those things that make them unique start to vanish. In the end, the victim falls under the total control of the narcissist and would do anything they desire.

Stages of Gaslighting in a Relationship

Gaslighting brings about an unhealthy power dynamic in a relationship, which is not easy for anyone to point out. The victim is urged to do the bidding of the gaslighter, which in this case, is a narcissist. Gaslighting can occur in society, workplaces, and even intimate relationships.

In this section, we will take an elaborate look into the stages of gaslighting in a relationship. However, depending on what's involved, the number of stages may differ, and so may their order. Nonetheless, below are some of the typical stages.

Exaggerate and Tell Lies

The narcissist gaslighter creates a story that is usually not true and negative about the victim. The goal of this is to make them feel that there is something wrong with them. The narcissist achieves this using fake stories as opposed to evidence-based facts, all of which places the victim on the defensive.

Recurrence

The narcissist gaslighter constantly recounts these false and negative facts they have created. This ensures the victim is always on the defensive, and the narcissist on the offensive, leaving them in control of the relationship the entire time.

Escalate When Their Lies Are Pointed Out

The moment the victim calls out the narcissist on their lies, they make the disagreement more intense by increasing the attacks. Besides, they challenge their lies with more fake stories, denials and blame, even with the evidence available. All of these are done to divert the victim's attention. This gives the narcissist the chance to input doubts and confusion in the victim's minds.

Wear Down the Victim

As the victim is constantly placed on the defensive, they soon become exhausted. In most situations, the victim begins to doubt themselves, become scared, and may become drained and submissive. Soon, the victim starts to doubt their views, perspectives, and who they are as individuals.

Develop Co-Dependent Relationships

When the victim has been worn down in the relationship, their constant self-doubt and anxiety allows the narcissist to manipulate them however they want. The narcissist can provide financial security, affection, and recognition and often threaten the victim that they will take it back anytime they want. With this fear and weakness, it leads to a co-dependent relationship.

Offer False Hope

To manipulate their victim, the narcissist may use kindness, fairness, and a promise of repentance to give the victim a false sense of hope. All of these will make the victims start to feel the narcissist is not so terrible and that they may change. These, along with many other similar thoughts, may cross the mind of the victim and confuse them further.

However, reality tends to set in with time as these acts of kindness and fairness are short-lived. The narcissist only uses them to make the victims lower their guard in preparation for the next act of gaslighting. With this technique, the abuser strengthens the co-dependent relationship even more.

Full Control

In most instances, the core objective of a narcissist who is also an obsessive gaslighter is to control and dominate someone else or other people. By continuously using falsehoods and intimidation, while gradually increasing the intensity, the narcissist can make certain that the victim is always scared, vulnerable, insecure, and dealing with self-doubt. After this has taken place, the narcissist can use the victim when they want in a manner that benefits them.

What Happens to You When You Are Abused?

Similar to other victims who experienced narcissistic abuse, you most likely never knew what you were dealing with until you had been left wondering why your partner suddenly morphed into the monster they are. You had become a shadow of your former self.

However, what many people have an even more difficult time pointing out is that narcissistic abuse tends to have an impact on their lives. This is the reason why you need to understand the major ways the behavior of the narcissist affects your life. In this chapter, we will be looking into some of the major ones, and if you are experiencing any of these in your life, it may be a clear sign that you need to get out of the relationship fast.

You Feel Alone Most Times

A relationship is meant to provide you with companionship and happiness down to the depths of your soul. However, if you always feel extremely lonely even when you have a partner you do everything with, then it is a clear effect of the narcissist. You may also find yourself daydreaming about someone to offer you the love you desire and get rid of feelings of intense loneliness you feel.

This is one of the major effects of narcissistic abuse in the life of a victim. Many of the victims are living in the illusion created by the narcissist that does not exist and may have been isolated from all of their friends and family members.

You Walk on Eggshells

This is another major sign that you are a victim of narcissistic abuse. Many victims tend to stay away from anything similar to the trauma they dealt with during the abuse. This could range from activities, locations, or individuals that seem like a danger to them.

Regardless if your narcissistic abuser is your coworker, friend, spouse or family member, you continuously tread carefully and monitor what you say and do around them so you aren't punished or incur their anger.

If you are like many other victims, you will find that this does not offer any results, and you will remain the best option for the abuser anytime they need someone to abuse. Because of this, you may be nervous about annoying or irritating your narcissistic abuser and may avoid creating boundaries or having any confrontation with them.

You become a people pleaser, and this may extend to other areas of your life, aside from your abusive relationship. In doing so, you lose your capacity to put your foot down when you need to, especially when dealing with other people who seem similar to your abuser and the abuse you have suffered.

You Prioritize the Desires of the Abuser

At some point, you may have had a life filled with goals, ambitions, and dreams. But now, it feels like everything about your life is centered around the narcissist. At this point, your whole life revolves around the narcissist, and you may have put aside all of your hobbies, goals, and friendships to make sure that your abuser is pleased with the relationship.

However, soon you find out that regardless of what you do, the narcissist abuser will always want more.

You Find It Hard to Trust Anyone

Trusting others is now very difficult, and any person you come across seems similar to the narcissist considering how nice they were before they betrayed your trust. Due to this, you become wary about anyone you come across and find it difficult to trust anyone, even yourself. This is also as a result of the constant gaslighting you have suffered that has resulted in you doubting yourself over the years.

You Deal with Suicidal Thoughts

Coupled with the constant nervousness and feeling of depression that comes along with narcissistic abuse, you may deal with a constant feeling of helplessness. Your daily experience is not a great one, and you don't feel you can cope anymore. To worsen things, you can't leave even if you wanted to. The helplessness you feel inside makes you feel like you want the day to be your last. Many victims may even pick up self-harm as a means of coping.

You Isolate Yourself

Normally, the narcissistic abuser isolates the victims. But there are instances where the victim may do the isolation by themselves because they feel shame concerning the abuse that they are dealing with. Due to the common trend in society where the victim is blamed for the abuse they go through, many victims would rather hide.

This is because they believe nobody will understand what they have experienced. Family, friends, and law enforcement may not acknowledge the abuse since it is usually emotional without any physical trace. They believe nobody will believe them, and instead of coming out, they isolate themselves to prevent further traumatization.

If you discover that you are keeping yourself away from the eye of the public, and have cut off contact with people you know, you may be dealing with narcissistic abuse.

You Compare Yourself with Others

Narcissists use triangulation to make their victims feel less and compete for their love. Due to this, victims possess the inner fear that they are inadequate and will always do all they can to get the approval and attention of the narcissist abuser.

Sometimes, victims may even compare their relationships to others around them who are much happier. They may often see their narcissist abuser treating others much better than they are treated and wonder why they deserve so much pain. This constant comparison can result in them blaming themselves for the abuse they have suffered. If you are dealing with this, you need to remember that the narcissist is to be blamed for their unhealthy behavior, and it is not your fault in any way for being abused.

You Sabotage Yourself

During the period of abuse, the narcissist abuser will always talk down on the victim and make them feel like they can amount to no good. This negative talk tends to keep replaying in the mind of the victim, even in the absence of the abuser. This constant negative voice in their head results in a pattern of self-sabotage and self-destruction.

Many victims tend to continuously carry the shame they feel and punish themselves at all times. This can result in suicide for many of these victims. Others are unable to achieve their set goals, desires, and aspirations because of the feeling of worthlessness the narcissist has implanted in them. They tend to believe they will fail even before they start any activity, and due to this negative thinking, they always do.

You Are Scared of Doing the Things You Enjoy or to be Successful

As noted earlier, narcissists want something that they lack from their victims. They are also jealous of their victims and tend to punish them anytime they attain success. These toxic individuals do this by conditioning their victims to link all of their hobbies, interests, and achievements with abuse. This makes victims feel that if they attain any form of success, they will have to deal with the pain of abuse.

Because of this, many victims cope with depression and may stay away from things that would give them attention, and this includes being successful. To free yourself from this fear, you need to realize that your abuser does not put you down because your talents are poor, but because they are envious of your capabilities as they could destroy the hold they have on you.

You Make Excuses for Your Abuser

A common survival mechanism many victims of abuse adopt is to tone down the seriousness of the abuse. To minimize the pain you feel when someone who claims to have an undying love for you is responsible for your abuse, many abuse victims will make excuses for their abuser. They may tell themselves that the abuser is not so bad or is experiencing issues beyond their control.

You need to understand that the narcissist you met at the start was only an illusion. The monster you know presently is the true narcissist. In addition to this, victims may have unhealthy trauma bonds with the narcissist abuser and will try to protect them from the consequences of their actions. To do this, they may pretend to outsiders that everything is fine and may even blame their clumsiness for the numerous scars and marks resulting from physical abuse. Some may even take part blame of the situation by saying they did something to trigger the abuse from the narcissist abuser.

You Start Portraying Unhealthy Behavior Toward Those Around You

When you are in a relationship with a narcissist, you are always at the receiving end of toxicity. You become a dumping ground for all of the negative feelings they don't want to handle, and at some point, you will require an outlet to dump it on too. Most times, due to the conditioning of the narcissist, victims are unable to dump the toxicity back to them, but instead, they find the next innocent person and portray those same unhealthy habits.

You never can tell which of your other relationships will be destroyed as a result of the abuse you have suffered. If you want to live a healthy life, you will need to rid yourself of this kind of relationship as quickly as you can.

Narcissistic Abuse and Your Health

In a healthy relationship, your health also gets a positive benefit. However, if your partner is always causing you constant pain and frustration, just as a narcissist does, it may harm your overall health, all of which did not exist before. You may even notice signs of aging, even though you are still young. Your stress level has gone up due to the constant abuse, and your immune system has been lowered, leaving you open to various diseases.

Every relationship has its rough patches, but those relationships involving a narcissist are ruled with pain and constant frustration, all of which can affect your health negatively in the following ways.

Inability to Sleep

Sleeping is also a problem due to the nightmares you have when you try to sleep, as all you can do is relive your abuse. In some other instances, the sleep you need never comes. All of this may result in picking up a lot of unhealthy habits that are also a detriment to your health. You may start to overeat, drink, smoke, and abuse substances as a way of battling the huge amount of stress you are dealing with. However, all of these may only provide a brief reprieve. Before you know it, you will be stuck in the unhealthy cycle of addiction coupled with the emotional sabotage that never stops.

It Can Lead to Unwarranted Weight Loss

When you are in a relationship that is riddled with problems, it can result in weight loss. As we previously stated, emotional problems can cause the inability to eat meals in the right amount, as consuming meals becomes a chore. Soon, the effects of not eating properly start to reflect on your body in the form of weight loss. In addition to this, you may also suffer from paleness that can cause you look physically older.

Elevated Stress Level

Excess stress is not ideal for the body, and the toxic relationship you share with a narcissist leads to a huge level of stress. Due to the constant unhappiness you feel, you are always anxiously anticipating the next argument and abuse. Your mind is always clouded with thoughts, and if you have other obligations, they can all merge to cause an insane amount of stress. Too much stress is unhealthy because it can also lead to personality disorders, heart attacks, and even stroke.

Headaches

Being in a toxic relationship with a narcissist can result in unending headaches due to the constant disagreements you have with your partner. Being in a state of constant argument with someone who claims to love you can take a toll on your overall health.

Chapter 4: Why Are You Attracting Narcissists?

It is not an easy task to remain in a relationship with a narcissist. You will have to continually walk on eggshells if you don't want to set off your partner. In most situations, being in a relationship with these individuals is not worth it. Even if they do not have the intention to cause you harm, their nature seems to seep out and cause problems in your relationship.

But what do you do when you don't have any intention to find these toxic individuals in the first place? What if they are the ones who find their way to you? How then do you handle it? For a good number of victims, this is the problem they face. They don't actively chase after these toxic individuals, but for some reason, these individuals tend to find them.

The reality is that if you are continually attracting narcissists, there is a behavior you are exhibiting that is drawing them to you. In other instances, you most likely have something they want to get from you. This could range from power, finances, or empathy.

Contrary to the belief of many people, narcissists do not go after weak individuals who they can manipulate with ease. Instead, narcissists chase people who have a strong will and possess traits that they desire. This way, they can boost their egos more when they can destroy the individual.

Since narcissistic people are always in search of ways to make themselves feel good, they have a higher tendency of seeking those who will help them do that. They either boost their egos by associating with them or by breaking them apart and taking complete control.

If you are constantly attracting narcissists, you need to know what you are doing so you can curb it and prevent yourself from getting continuously stuck with these individuals. But before we move any further, we will be taking a more in-depth look at why narcissists are drawn to certain individuals.

Why Narcissists are Attracted to Certain People

Narcissists are drawn to individuals who possess something they desire. This could be mental, physical, material, or emotional needs. The kind of person a narcissist wants at a given moment is dependent on their immediate desire.

In addition to this, the narcissist also has a role to play. For example, covert narcissists may be attracted to extremely empathic individuals. This is because these individuals can offer them the type of understanding and sensitivity they are after. An overt individual, on the other hand, may be in search of someone they can control completely. A person who leaves all the decision-making to them. It could also be an individual who has attained a level of success or is physically appealing so that the narcissist can use them as a way to feel good. Regardless of the kind of narcissist involved, the core goal is to look for an ideal partner for their requirements.

Narcissists have a script for how they want their relationships to go. However, this is one of the primary reasons their relationships do not last. The expectations they have are put to life in this script, and it is always unrealistic. Due to how silly their expectations are, things never go as planned. For this reason, they tend to be disappointed that their partner is not following the script they have put in place. This makes them feel bitter that they do not have the ideal partner. And since they don't know how to portray their emotions appropriately, they tend to react with betrayal, rage, and bitterness. For this reason, narcissists are more attracted to those who they feel can offer them the ideal relationship they want.

Those who remain in relationships with narcissists are usually compassionate and empathetic individuals. In addition, these individuals may have some specific gift or talent, all of which the narcissist is jealous of. The narcissist usually has the opposite of these qualities and feels that if they get a partner who has them, they can also tap from all of it.

This is usually the primary goal of the narcissist, but because they are unable to actually feel some of these emotions, or don't have these talents, they tend to become bitter. The narcissist believes in creating an illusion until it becomes a reality, but it never comes to fruition.

After they have come to accept that they can't make these qualities on their own, they start to grow a deep feeling of jealousy and look for ways to eradicate all these qualities in their partner. To the narcissist, doing this will ensure nobody possesses them.

Take the story of two kids, for example. John met Mark on the playground with a toy car he wanted to play with. However, when he tried to play with the toy car, Mark refused, and this made John jealous. Out of envy, he deliberately wrecked Mark's car, and that left him in tears. However, John was not bothered about the way Mark felt because the object that was causing the problem had been eradicated. This is a similar example of how narcissists act in reality.

If their partner was very good at dancing and the narcissist lacked in this area, they would look for ways to undermine and even destroy this talent. For instance, they might say that the victim's dancing isn't spectacular and that people are only pretending to like it.

Since the narcissist is unable to get these qualities for themselves, they take this route either to make their partner feel bad about having them or completely let go. To a narcissist, the perfect partner would be one who was a fantastic dancer but informed everyone that the narcissist was much better. Their ideal partner is one who undermines their talents to make the narcissist feel good.

Having learned this, what are the possible reasons you could be attracting narcissists in your life? Below are a few of the most probable reasons.

You Are Lonely and Hate Being Alone

Grace had never been single for too long. As soon as one relationship ended, she was in another. She did not enjoy being alone and ensured it did not happen. However, after her last breakup, she was unable to get into a new relationship for a year, and at this point, she was starting to get desperate. She just wanted someone she could call her own, regardless of who the person was. Soon, Jack came along. He was charismatic and amazing, and before long, she was drawn in. However, Jack began to show his true colors, as he continually shamed and abused Grace throughout the relationship. Grace noticed all of these traits, but instead of leaving, she stayed because the idea of being alone was much worse than dating a narcissist.

This behavior is specifically why Jack was drawn to Grace. If you are anything like Grace, a narcissist can sense it.

They understand that the lonely person is willing to do anything to avoid loneliness. And soon, the narcissist transforms it into a weapon that they can use against their victim. If you can't stand the idea of being alone, it will become evident in your behavior, and it will make you an ideal prey for the narcissist.

You Are Smart or Talented

Like we have stated earlier, narcissists don't prey on weak people. Instead, they prefer someone with a trait they can benefit from. If you are smart, you will become extremely attractive to a narcissist, who will likely approach you. The reason for this is simple; it is a massive boost to their ego when they break down someone smart.

The same is the case if you are talented and have a specific skill they can boost their ego with. Narcissists always want a quality they do not have and will be drawn to those they believe possess these qualities they can tap from.

Many smart and talented people feel ashamed for not spotting narcissists until it is too late. But remember that it is not your fault. These toxic individuals are experienced at what they do and know the right words to reel you in. So let go of the self-blame and learn from your past experiences.

You are Extremely Empathic

Narcissists believe that they are better than everyone else. This leads to an urge for respect, attention, and fame without any form of empathy for how their desires affect other people around them. This brings about people who are willing to step on others and use them to get what they want.

In comparison, empathic individuals are caring and thoughtful. They are the complete opposite of a narcissist, but this does not stop them from attracting the narcissist. Why is this so?

By now, you should know that a narcissist doesn't show their true selves when they first approach their victim. In fact, they use all forms of manipulation techniques to keep up the façade. They tend to reel in their victim with this behavior before showing their true colors later on. If a typical person notices it, he or she is more likely to pick up his bags and leave the narcissist behind.

However, for someone who is empathic, this is not the same. People with an extreme level of empathy have an ever-increasing urge to take care of others and help them. And since the narcissist is a person who needs constant admiration, care, support, validation and reassurance, and frequent bouts of disappointment and anger, the empathic person is urged to help them.

This is because these extremely empathic people tend to understand the pain of others and may have the urge to help them. They are usually at the forefront when someone needs to be consoled, and this is why the narcissist is drawn to them. These toxic individuals are aware of this and take full advantage of their empathy by enjoying constant love, care, and compassion. On the other hand, the individual with empathy may be continuously drained and will deal with various forms of abuse, projection, and so on.

In addition, empathic individuals hardly call out the narcissist on their behavior. They would rather empathize with them instead because they feel some of the behavior of the narcissist is their fault. For this reason, many extremely empathic individuals end up protecting the narcissist so they don't deal with any of the repercussions.

Narcissists understand all of this and know that those who are incredibly empathic are more likely to keep up with them and their unhealthy behavior. If you are someone who always needs to understand others and care for them, then it may be why you are attracting narcissists.

You are Highly Sentimental

Do you love the idea of romance? Or do you dream about that perfect relationship and that there is a soul mate? Or perhaps you read meaning into the smallest of gestures? If you responded yes to all of these, then you probably are a sentimental individual, and narcissists are attracted to people like you.

The narcissist can spot those who are highly sentimental and can reel them in using their need for gestures and love. They do these at the beginning of the relationship to get the sentimental person to trust them completely.

Even when the narcissist starts to show their true colors later in the relationship, the sentimental partner holds on to the early memories. This is what sees them through all of the abuse instead of leaving, and the narcissists tend to capitalize on this behavior.

You are Resilient

Are you able to find your bearing and keep forging ahead after an experience that would keep others down? Do you always see challenges as a way to grow yourself? If yes, then this is a trait that narcissists find appealing.

These characteristics are not terrible to have because for one to navigate through life, he or she has to be resilient.

However, in the hands of the narcissist, this resilience can be a weapon. Narcissists can use the strength of a person to trap them in the constant abuse they dish out. Since resilient people know how to keep forging on, they have a lower tendency to leave a relationship with the narcissist even when things aren't going well. Instead of leaving, they would go the notion that things will get better, and it is only a rough patch.

Due to this type of thinking, they may try to solve the problems in their relationship by playing the role of the savior. There are cases of resilient individuals who use the amount of pain they can withstand to determine how much they love their partners, leaving them in relationships longer than they should.

You Grew Up in a Toxic Environment

The way you were raised can influence your life. This is the case, regardless of the kind of experience you have had. If you were raised by a narcissist, then there is a huge possibility that you may have developed unhealthy traits that would draw more narcissists to you as an adult.

Even if you were to come across a narcissist, you would be less likely to leave, even with the abuse, because this behavior had become normal for you while growing up. Other ways you were raised that can make you attract narcissists include:

You Have the Urge to Fix Others

Because you have been raised by a narcissist, you may have groomed the idea of fixing others and focusing on them while letting go of your own needs. This seemingly obsessive behavior can make you a suitable prey for a narcissist who wants someone to focus on them and their desires.

However, the goal of fixing these toxic individuals never comes true, leaving the fixer stuck in a relationship trying to achieve a goal that will never be achieved.

You Have Become a People Pleaser

One of the major effects of being raised in a home with narcissists is that you transform into a people pleaser. If, as a child, the only way you were able to get attention from your parents was to do what they wanted, you may associate it with other parts of your life. It is also a behavior that is extremely difficult to break free of.

Someone who behaves this way is a perfect partner for the narcissist. They generally stay away from conflicts and would do anything possible to keep the peace in their relationship. This means they are willing to allow the narcissist to take complete control and walk over them. If you are a people pleaser, you will have an easy time drawing a narcissist in your direction.

In addition to people-pleasing, there is also an extension, and that is the need to get approval from others. This is similar to what the narcissist does, and if you have this trait, you will easily attract narcissists to your life.

Because they are attuned to this kind of desire, they see people with the same need as someone they could tap from with ease. To get them attached, they will use validation and tons of attention before they use it against you later.

You Don't Feel Loveable

This is another major effect of being raised in an unhealthy environment. With time, an individual starts to feel unlovable and that they do not matter.

For the narcissist who believes that they are better than everyone else and only their needs matter, those who already feel this way would make great targets for them. All they need to do is swoon in and continue fueling this impression they already have to their benefit.

Emotional and Psychological Reasons Why Victims Stay in a Relationship with a Narcissist

People who have not experienced a narcissistic relationship are always confused as to why those in this type of relationships stay. They wonder why the abused person doesn't leave the abuser.

However, people get stuck for various reasons, and these reasons may be complicated for those on the outside to understand. In fact, it is not something that can easily be explained. So why then do people still stay in these kinds of relationships even with the damage it causes? We will cover some of these reasons in this section so you can determine if you have the same reasons for remaining in an unhealthy relationship.

They Don't Know Any Better

Those who were raised in homes where abuse was the order of the day soon believed this was the norm. So, when they get stuck in a relationship where abuse is prominent, they see it as normal. They grew up without getting love from their parents, so even with a narcissistic partner who doesn't love them, they don't feel any differently. This is what they know and have associated as normal, so they live with it.

In other cases, many individuals do not even know that they are in an unhealthy relationship. They don't know how to recognize a narcissist, and they don't have any family or friends who have been in a relationship with one and passed on information. For many people, the earliest examples of healthy relationships are from their parents and the adults around them. Sadly, for many people, the adults around them weren't in healthy relationships to relay what it's like to be in one.

These individuals grow into adults with the wrong ideas of what a relationship should be and remain stuck with a narcissist feeling that the abuse and control is normal. If you take a look into your life presently and you are unable to determine the difference between a healthy and unhealthy relationship, then this is a red flag. Still, you don't have to feel bad about this or blame yourself, but take steps to move further and learn the differences.

They Don't Feel Like They Deserve Better

Many people who remain with a narcissist in an unhealthy relationship do so because they don't believe they deserve better. These people feel that what they are getting is what they deserve, and they won't find better outside. If you remain in an unhealthy relationship like that involving a narcissist, you are only letting them know that it is okay for them to treat you the way they are doing.

But if you can summon the courage to let go of this kind of relationship, you will be letting them know that you are no pushover, and you know your self-worth. It is also letting them know that you are capable of choosing the best option for you.

They are Scared

It will be surprising to note that many people stay in a relationship with the narcissist because they are scared. They are afraid of being judged, ridiculed, and losing all of the benefits they gain from the relationship.

Many of them ask questions like: What will my friends say? How do I go forward when I leave them? How do I cater to my financial needs that were previously covered by my partner?

These types of individuals are scared of a huge number of variables, which makes it very difficult for them to leave.

They Don't Want to Hurt Their Partners

This is the case mostly for individuals with empathy. These individuals care more about how others feel. Many people have empathy, but those who are extremely empathic are willing to go further than other typical individuals when it comes to showing care and understanding for others.

However, as you know by now, empathy is a characteristic that narcissists tend to take advantage of. Because they don't want to cause any harm to their partner by leaving, they tend to postpone the break up and ignore the level of pain it is causing them. This way, they may remain in an unhealthy relationship longer than needed.

They are Hoping Things will Change

This is common among resilient people. These types of individuals are used to forging ahead with the hope that things will get better. However, this is a deadly way to think when in a relationship with a narcissist. Instead of things getting better, it never does because narcissists are unable to change who they are. For this reason, these individuals may remain stuck in this type of unhealthy relationship for many years.

Also, individuals with this kind of belief are more likely to find excuses for these partners, even with serious abuse. They make up excuses such as financial or work problems. Rather than see their partners for who they are, they forge on believing that the instant these partners get past the problems they are dealing with, they will change, and things will get better. However, in the case of a narcissist, this is something that never happens.

They Are Accustomed to Pain

When you continuously expose yourself to a situation, the more you build resistance to it and see it as normal. The same is also when it involves unhealthy relationships and the abuse that comes with it. The more time you spend in a relationship with a narcissist filled with pain, frustration, and abuse, the more likely you are to grow accustomed to it.

With time, you see everything you face as normal and make no move to free yourself from the situation. Instead of looking for a way to engage in a healthy relationship, you stay in the present one.

They Stay for the Sake of the Kids

As a parent, it is natural to do everything possible to ensure your kids have the best in life. However, for people who extend this train of thought, this can be a huge drawback.

Separation or divorce leads to disruption for children, and for parents who want to avoid this, they may remain in an abusive relationship thinking that it's what's best for the kids. What they don't realize is that they are actually teaching their children that abuse is okay, and that to accept abuse as a way of life is also okay.

It is an unhealthy environment for the children, and while the victim feels they are doing what's best, they are harming not only themselves but their children. If the narcissistic behavior escalates to physical violence, both the victim and the children could be in grave danger.

If this is your situation, leave while you can. If you have no place to go, you can always find safety and shelter at the nearest domestic violence shelter.

They Are Being Manipulated

The narcissist is known to manipulate their victim at every given chance. Soon, they gain control over every aspect of their partner's life. This is the case for many people who are in a relationship with a narcissist. These people are in the relationship because the narcissist is manipulating them to believe they will regret ending the relationship.

A narcissist will point out the many reasons why you need to remain in the relationship. They will remind you of why you need them. Whether it's financial or because of children, they will load their partner up with all the bad things that could happen if they leave.

A bad situation would be if the victim is dependent on the narcissist for employment. If the narcissist owns a company and the victim works for the company, that's a hold that can easily be manipulated.

They Have No Means of Leaving

A lot of people get stuck with narcissistic partners because they have no way to leave. Some people may not be able to leave because they don't have the needed finances, and some may not have anyone to support them. Even when they are tired of the relationship and want to leave, the fear of the unknown makes them remain in the relationship.

Without friends and family to turn to for support, they tend to give up even before they try. They may know that the happiness and peace they desire is outside their relationship with the narcissist, but they may not have the courage, support, and strength to carry on with it.

They No Longer Have Any Hope

Dealing with constant abuse can eat deeply into the being of a person. The narcissist is also able to gaslight victims until they no longer trust themselves. With time, they give up on all of their desires and have no hope for a better life.

These types of individuals are the opposite of resilient people as they have already resigned to fate and believe that the future is bleak. All of these thoughts may lead to this individual remaining in a relationship with the narcissist, even with the obvious damage it is causing them.

They Feel Guilty

Narcissists are masters of manipulation, and they can manipulate their victims into believing they are responsible for anything negative in the relationship. They are well-versed at playing the victim and blaming their partner for all of their abusive behaviors. The narcissist may make them believe that their compliant and nagging is stressing them out. And soon, the victim may start to believe the statements of the narcissists, resulting in a feeling of guilt.

When a victim is blamed for events that occur whenever they try to speak to their partner, it could lead to a reduction in self-esteem and an increase in guilt. If this takes place frequently, it becomes hard for the victim to have a reasonable conversation with their narcissistic partner.

If this is the situation that you are going through, remember that you are not to blame even though the narcissist has conditioned you to believe you are.

They Are Afraid of Being Alone

Loneliness can be scary, and many of us would rather not spend our time alone. This is understandable as humans are social creatures who need to interact with others. However, when your happiness is dependent on the presence of someone else, then it becomes a problem.

This is the case for many victims. Their lives have become completely centered around their narcissistic partner that the thought of leaving them is unbearable. They believe that the relationship they have with the narcissist partner is a chance that many would die for, and they do everything possible to make certain that they don't lose it.

However, being alone is not as scary as it seems. It is a great time to reflect and think of ways to improve yourself. Also, if you can enjoy your company, then it will be less difficult for others to enjoy it too. Doing this will make it less likely for you to be dependent on anyone for your happiness.

You can also use the time alone to learn more about narcissistic relationships so that you can point them out from afar. When you can do this, you can then find individuals who will give you the healthy relationship you deserve, which will be less difficult since you now have a direction.

Chapter 5: Leaving A Narcissist - Things You Should Know

It can be terrifying to leave a narcissist. Even though it is the healthy and sensible thing for you to do, it can be a scary path to take. In fact, it will probably be one of the scariest things you do. This is the reason why many victims stay stuck in the relationship.

Having any type of relationship with a narcissist is bound to be traumatic. However, this does not mean your trauma will end as soon as you get the narcissist out of your life. Below, we will be looking into some of the most vital things you need to know when it comes to leaving these toxic beings.

There are After-Effects

Take the story of Daisy, for instance. She had been in a relationship with Mark for over five years. All through the relationship, she suffered various forms of abuse until she could no longer take it anymore. She soon decided it was time to leave and took the bold step of leaving her abuser of five years. However, what she did not plan for was the pain she felt immediately after she ended the relationship. It was so overwhelming, and when she couldn't take it anymore, she went back to Mark. At that point, being with him was much better than the pain she felt from staying away from him.

Daisy's story is the story of many victims who leave a narcissistic relationship. Most people fail to plan for the after-effects of leaving. However, it is one of the most important things you need to wrap your head around before you take this leap.

When you end your relationship with the narcissist, it does not mean you will automatically be fine. On some rare occasions, this might happen, but it is implausible. The reason for this is the unhealthy trauma bond the victim creates with the narcissist after many years of abuse.

Think of the narcissist as an alcoholic drink or drug you are addicted to. The instant you stop being around them, your body begins to react violently. This is usually not evident when you are around the narcissist, and it only crops up when you leave.

These feelings that come up at this point are usually much worse than what you feel when in the relationship. It will seem like you can't live an extra day without reaching out to this person, and many people tend to confuse this as love, which is why they go back to the narcissist in most cases.

Feeling like your life cannot go on anymore when someone is not in the picture can be very frustrating, and it may be tempting to go back. You need to understand that the feelings that come after you leave are going to be painful, so you need to be ready for it. This is because it is one of the major things that can take you off the course of recovery.

The Narcissist Does Not Care About Understanding

When you decide to leave, the narcissist will do everything possible to make it as difficult as possible. They will use all the tricks in their arsenal to ensure you suffer and pay for leaving them. To the narcissist, you are the one with all the faults, and this means you have to pay. They achieve this by shaming, demeaning, and abusing you as much as they can.

You may feel like you have to fix your relationship with the narcissist to fix the barrage of attacks that come your way. However, this is part of it, and you need to be prepared. If whatever the narcissist does after you leave begins to trigger you into acting in anger or frustration, you will be doing exactly what they want, and the attacks will never stop.

The more the effort you make trying to get closure, and let the narcissist know your point of view, the more they increase the abuse. With the abuse, you will try to engage by justifying or defending yourself, but the abuse will only get worse.

The moment the abuse begins, ignore it and do not engage in it in any manner. Remain calm, and do not be triggered no matter what the narcissist throws your way. This way, the narcissist will no longer have any power over you or your life.

Plan Your Exit

By now, you know how terrible the narcissist can be. They can do everything in their power to make certain that leaving them is frustrating for you. Sometimes, they may carry out steps to make your leaving futile and unsuccessful. This means you have to be smart when leaving. To make sure your exit goes the way it should, it is crucial for you to have a rock-solid plan.

Below are a few things you can put in place before you leave.

- **Put a Safety Plan in Place**: If you are dealing with an extremely violent partner, this will be essential. A scorned abusive narcissistic individual is not predictable, and even if you feel the person is not a problem, you will still need to make plans for your safety. Prioritize your safety by putting a plan in place with an expert or someone close to you.

  Look for a safe location that your abusive partner does not know of. This becomes increasingly important if there are kids involved. To make certain that the location you choose is secure, your best bet is not to tell anyone about your plans, except some trustworthy family members. This is because some of your loved ones who care about you may mistakenly tell your narcissist partner where you are located. They may not know how serious the problem is and may be doing it to help. However, the outcome of their interference may turn out negative instead of positive.

- **Have Proper Records:** Many narcissists, as you know, will hardly let go of their partners with ease. To get them back, they may contact them and resort to manipulation, abuse, and threats to achieve this. This is where the No Contact strategy can be of help. (We will look into this strategy in detail later in this book.)

  If your former narcissist partner reaches out to you, make certain that you keep a record of all the conversations and threats. Each of these will be essential if you ever go to court.

- **File for a Restraining Order if Needed**: If you feel your life or that of your kids may be in danger, this is a great option. Filing for a restraining order will have it on record that there is a threat to your life and also keep them far away from you.

Get your Finances Together

Narcissistic partners may sometimes resort to financial abuse, particularly if you are about to leave. They are fast to make sure you are unable to get your hands on funds if needed and close joint accounts. This means you need to have some finances in place to fall back on before you decide to leave.

Below, we will be looking at some ways to make this possible.

- **Establish a New Bank Account**: Open new bank accounts, especially if you have a joint account with your partner. This will be ideal for the future. If your partner knows your former accounts and can access them, you may want to contact your bank to help you change your security questions to something only you know. This will make certain that only you have access to the account. If you have items that are of value in a joint deposit box, you can open one of your own in another bank. Take out your essential items and place them in the new one. You can also place all your essential documents and items in the safety deposit box.

- **Ramp up your savings**: It will be important to have some money in your account before you decide to leave. It is best to use the account you created above. In addition to this, you may want to get some credit cards as well. These will be extremely useful if the need to leave quickly arises. Also, if you have a job, you could speak to your HR to send a part of your payment to another account automatically. Your HR can also help you make changes to your W-4 so you can save or invest more. There are many ways you can save; all you need to do is to pick one that works for you.

- **Take out a loan:** If possible, take out a loan if you have no other means of cash. You can get a bank loan borrow from a family member or a friend. Make certain that your partner can't learn of it. For example, if you take a bank loan, be sure to tell your lender of your situation so that you can ensure that no information is released about your finances.

- **Make Copies of Your Important Documents**: Make copies of all your vital documents, especially those that have to do with your finances. This could include tax returns, bank statements, investment statements, and loan information. You can also scan them and upload them on a personal Google drive or the cloud. This way, you can print out copies of these documents from any location.

- **Reach out to a Financial Advisor**: The services of a financial advisor is also significant. An expert can show you how you can cut down your costs and channel more to your savings. If you presently share an account with your partner, take steps to find one of your own. If you can't afford an expert, you can check out your local library and the internet for financial classes. Members of your family and close friends, coworkers, among others, who are well-versed in everything that has to do with money, can only be of help.

- **Remove Your Name from Joint Credit Cards:** This is important. You want to remove yourself from all joint credit cards, and if the card is in your name and your partner is an authorized user, be sure to remove them right away. You can also cancel the cards and get new account numbers. You want to be certain to sever all financial ties. A narcissist can do a lot of damage to the victim's credit if they seek revenge. Be prepared and break all financial times to avoid a mess down the road.

Chapter 6: How to Heal from Emotional Abuse

At this point, you know how excruciating the emotional abuse one suffers in the hands of narcissists can be. This type of abuse destroys one from the inside and can affect your mental health and individuality for years to come.

This is why it takes a while for one to heal from this form of abuse. Since the damage has to do with the mind, it is one that requires a different approach to heal from. The majority of the work lies in the hands of you as the victim because you will need to cleanse all of the conditioning carried out by the narcissist in your mind before you can get the recovery you need. But before we go any further, let us take a look at why it is different to heal from narcissistic abuse.

Why is Difficult to Heal from Narcissistic Abuse in Comparison to Others?

The trauma that comes from narcissistic abuse can be likened to fighting a consistent battle where your mental, emotional, and physical body is being attacked for years. The impact on the psychology of the victim is enormous.

After dealing with non-wavering abuse for a long time, the victim starts to wonder why peace is difficult to attain when others are living fine. Then the notion that something is wrong with them crops up, as they believe this is why the abuse continues.

Narcissistic abuse is like a traumatic event, which is why recovery is different. It attacks your spirit, person, and your sense of self.

How Does Narcissistic Abuse Affect You on a More Profound Level?

Narcissistic abuse usually occurs when a healthy individual is trying to have a healthy relationship with a person who is not capable of love. It is the way the dysfunctional person reacts during an intimate relationship.

As a result of the well-timed and strategically utilized manipulation techniques the narcissist has in their arsenal, and the victim develops an unhealthy trauma bond with the narcissist. During the first episode of argument and harmful verbal abuse, the victim may overlook it as a one-time occurrence.

However, the fighting and argument get more frequent, and the victim soon finds out that regardless of what they do and how they handle matters, they are never right.

The narcissist must always be the one who has been wronged no matter what, and with time, the victim begins to believe this genuinely, and the self-blame arises even without them knowing it. Narcissistic abuse affects the victim and everyone close to them. They soon start to think that they are irrelevant and can't do anything right. This feeling of worthlessness, combined with sadness and frustration makes narcissistic abuse affect victims differently.

Knowing the effect of this abuse, and the fact that it can last for many years, how then does one recover the right way? Below, we will be looking at some steps that can ensure this is seamless.

Steps to Help You Recover from Emotional Abuse of the Narcissist

Go No Contact

The first thing you need to do to recover is to get far away from the cause of your abuse. Regardless if it is your parent or lover, the steps remain the same. Then, after you have given them the needed distance, the next step is to cut all forms of communication with them. Many victims make the mistake of keeping the lines of communication open, and this allows narcissists to try to reel them in for another dose of abuse.

Others may try to reach out to the narcissist in a bid to have closure, but this never works. The narcissist has no reason for being the way they are, and neither do they have an explanation for their behavior. This means that even if you do reach out to them, you are most likely not going to learn anything meaningful.

Let us use the life of Drake as an example. He grew up with a narcissistic mother who continuously put him down and criticized him at every opportunity. When he grew older, he began to see how unhealthy being around his mother was, and in a bid to get better, he moved far away from the city where she lived. However, he still had a soft spot for his mother and made the mistake of leaving the lines of communication open. Soon, his mother began with the constant calls and texts, claiming one illness or the other all to bring him back home so she could continue to control him and make his life miserable. Drake gave into one of her calls, and even though he did not spend a day with her, the memories came flooding in, and he was back to where he started in regard to his recovery.

If Drake had cut off every means of communication or at least limited the communication outlet, this would not have been a problem. If you are serious about healing from emotional abuse, you need to get as far away from the source of your abuse as possible. The narcissist is the source in this case, and it does not make any difference if this narcissist is someone you feel is extremely close to you. For those who were in a relationship with a narcissist and managed to leave, they were tricked into meeting up one last time and manipulated into returning to the relationship. This is usually how it goes for a lot of victims.

In essence, if you are serious about your recovery, you need to make sure that the narcissist is not a part of your world anymore. This means no contact in any way regardless of if it via email, calls, or physical meetings. If you feel this is a tough call to make, remember the abuse you suffered and the potential for a repeat if you give in to the narcissist.

If you feel the narcissist is someone you can't do without in your life, such as a parent, then a good option will be to limit your contact with them. Give them only a single and less intrusive way to reach you in the event of emergencies. This could be via an email address you don't use frequently or an alternate phone number. Even if they do contact you, try to keep the conversation friendly and simple. Avoid going into details of your life even if they try to find out more about you.

This means communicate with them as if they were a casual associate.

You may also need to get rid of mutual friends as well. Narcissists, being the master manipulators that they are, may leverage mutual friends as a way to get you back into the relationship. These friends may unknowingly fill you in on what is going on in the life of the narcissist and their new conquests. This could breed jealousy, especially if you were in an intimate relationship with the narcissist. Some may even try to make you see why cutting off contact with the narcissist in your life is not a great idea and how much better your life would be with them in it. Do not fall for it, especially if you are serious about getting the recovery you desire.

If the narcissist was your lover, don't use the fantastic memories you have from the start of the relationship as an excuse to go back. If you do return to the relationship, you will be right back to where you started, dealing with the effects of the abuse in your life.

If you had children together and interaction isn't avoidable, you can get the help of an experienced mediator who can work up a parenting plan for you and the narcissist partner. This plan will cover financial sharing and visitation times so they can remain in the lives of the kids. It will also consist of an acceptable form of communication for both parties. This will give you the chance to pick a less intrusive option for the narcissist to reach you if necessary.

The bottom line is that if you are serious about getting better, and finding the recovery you need, going no contact is the best choice for you.

Do you Need to Tell the Narcissist That There will be No Contact?

It is not necessary to tell the narcissist that you desire no contact. The reason for this is simple—when you do, they may use it as a weapon against you. If you do tell them, ensure you are cutting off communication immediately after. Failure to do this will give the narcissist a chance to act in a bid to hold you back. They may do something harmful, which gets a reaction from you and leave you defending yourself until you find yourself stuck back in their abusive cycle once more.

Since your goal is to get out of the abusive cycle, you want to do everything to ensure this does not happen. Going no contact means you already understand how harmful the narcissist is to your health, and you have decided to say enough. It means you know that the healthiest option for you is to end the relationship because it is only going to get worse, and there is no longer any need to try.

Having no contact is a way to show you love yourself enough to get rid of anything that jeopardizes your sanity, which in this case, is the narcissist. This means there is no harm in going no contact without telling the narcissist anything about it. Sometimes, actions offer the best result.

The Wrong Reasons to go No Contact

Even though having no contact is very efficient, there is a right reason to do it. Some victims approach this strategy using the wrong mindset. For some individuals, no contact is a way to pay the narcissist back for all of the abuse they meted out to them over the years. For some, it is a way to make the narcissist see what they are missing, and perhaps the damage they have done so they would come back begging for forgiveness.

All of these are understandable, but it is not the right way to use the no contact rule. Using it this way only implies that you are still holding on to the illusion of the narcissist, and you are not prepared to heal.

Not having contact is not a game people play in relationships to get power over their partners, neither is it one that you use to change the narcissist.

You need to be completely honest with yourself if you want to make any headway. If your goal is to make your abuser feel pain, then it is a sign that you still want to save your relationship. This means you are not ready to free yourself from the abusive cycle.

The narcissist is a master of manipulation, which means you should not try to beat them at what they know best. You will end up the loser and probably be stuck in a life of more abuse.

If your goal is to use No Contact for revenge, there are a few ways it could turn out that include:

- The narcissist sees the error in their ways and gets back together with you. However, this may not last long as the relationship goes back to its regular pattern.
- You start to become more like the narcissist by using manipulation to get ahead in your relationships. This could cause you problems down the road.

In essence, only use the No Contact strategy if you are serious about getting over the narcissist and the abuse you have suffered. If this is not the case, it means you have a lot of work to do on yourself. Emotional damage is extremely painful and may require the help of an expert to deal with.

Cutting off contact does not have a time frame. However, it is not something that will be effective if you do it for a few days or weeks. It is something that you may have to do indefinitely. The reason is that if you allow the narcissist to reach you, they will continuously try to bug you until you start to feel frustrated. Besides, their being around constantly will keep the memories of the damage lingering.

If you do let them back into your life, they will wreak havoc and dump you once more.

Recover from the Self-Blame

The narcissist may have conditioned you to believe that their behavior is a result of something you did. Because of this, you may be dealing with constant self-blame. However, you need to remember that this is not the case as the narcissist has no empathy and is not capable of genuinely loving anyone. This is in no way your fault, and you need to understand this.

You are perfect, you are not worthless, and nothing is wrong with you.

You may also have learned to blame yourself when things don't go how you feel they should, even when it is not your fault. This is something you need to let go of as it is something that has been implanted in your head by the narcissist. This conditioning is something that has taken place over numerous years, and you need to break free from it.

This means you need to be kind to yourself and get rid of the self-blame because it is only slowing down your recovery. To show kindness to yourself, try the following:

- See yourself as your closest friend, and treat yourself in a similar manner.
- Anytime the urge to blame yourself comes up, remind yourself that this is what the narcissist is making you do, and it is not from you.
- Don't hide your feelings, instead acknowledge them and let it go. We will cover this in more detail later.

The moment you start to show kindness to yourself, you can now move on to recovering from the illusion of the narcissist.

Recover from The Illusion of the Narcissist

You may still be holding on to the illusion the narcissist has created and planted in your head, and if you are serious about getting the recovery you want, you will need to break this illusion.

The narcissist is charming and appealing to most victims when they meet them, and this is what many of them hold on to throughout the numerous years of abuse. This means there is a huge possibility that you are holding on to this illusion, as well.

First, you need to learn that it was only a façade the narcissist put up to reel you in. You need to let go of this illusion and see the narcissist for the unloving individuals that they are. Dreaming and holding on to this illusion and creating excuses for these toxic people won't get you anywhere. These individuals are damaged and are never going to change, regardless of how much you hold on to the illusion they have created.

By breaking the illusion of the narcissist in your life, you will be able to awaken your intuition, which you have been trained to doubt and start to benefit from its full power. As the fake world the narcissist has built around you falls apart, you soon begin to see the situation with more clarity. Remember that to move forward, you have to break down the fake structures that have been erected in your life. In time, you will reap the rewards.

The instant you can break free of the illusion, you can see them for the people they are and accept it.

Recover from Pain and Feeling of Loss

Regardless of how much abuse the narcissist dished out to you, they were still a considerable part of your life at some point. After living with a person and loving them for many years, you would undoubtedly have grown accustomed to them. This is why even when you decide to eradicate them from your life, there is still a massive void of pain where they used to be.

This is another essential step in your recovery. You need to let go of the feeling of loss you are experiencing. The narcissist does not deserve your love, and there is no benefit wallowing in pain and the sense of loss.

To do this, you will need to grieve the loss so you can feel better and move forward with your healing. There is no correct means of grieving, so you are allowed to pick a method you think works best for you. You can try painting or writing, as it has been said that activities that require your hands are great ways to heal.

Understandably, you were unable to get the attention and love from someone you loved, and this may cause some pain and feelings of loss lingering. Try to acknowledge these feelings and let them go.

By the time you have been able to grieve the right way, you can then move to the next stage of recovery.

Release the Fear of the Narcissist

The narcissist understands how powerful fear is and uses it to keep victims in check at all times. Many victims stay for so long in the relationship with the narcissist because of fear that has been embedded over the years.

As a victim, you are scared of the unknown, you are afraid of being alone, and you are scared of the wrath of the narcissist. The sad thing about all of these fears is that they remain there even after you have cut off the narcissist from your life. The fear still lingers and makes it extremely difficult to recover entirely from the damage that has been done to you.

You are scared of facing the world alone, and you are afraid of facing new challenges because the narcissist has made you believe that you will mess it up, and you are nothing without them. They have also conditioned you to associate punishment with any of your achievements, which makes you scared of attaining success anywhere you are. All of these are not real and have only been ingrained in you by the narcissist as a means to control you.

The narcissist is skilled at making you seem that you have no power over your life, and this is what keeps them in control. You need to understand that you alone have the power to make choices in your life and get the life you desire. You have made a choice to recover from the abuse, and you made the choice to cut off contact with the narcissist. You have the power, so stop letting the fear of the narcissist tie you down. The moment you can understand this and break free of this mental bondage, you can move to the next step of your recovery.

Recover and Heal the Need to Take Responsibility for the Narcissist

During your relationship with the narcissist, they may have made it seem like it's your responsibility to cater to their every need and desire. At some point, you may have even let go of aspirations, dreams, and goals of your own to cater to those of the narcissist.

This feeling has become a part of you since it is something you did for a good number of years. Even though you have decided to leave the narcissist behind and heal from the abuse you have suffered all through the years, there is still a good chance that this need for being responsible for the narcissist still lingers somewhere in your head.

Now is the time to let go and give priority to all of your needs and desires instead. At this point, only you matter, and that is where your priorities should lie.

Release the Connection to the Narcissist

There is an invisible bond that connects you to the narcissist even after you have let go. This connection functions to continuously zap your energy and leaves you feeling empty, lost, frustrated and out of control.

If you are serious about healing yourself, then you need to sever this connection and stop your energy from being continuously drained. There are a few ways you can sever this connection, and some of them include:

- **Eradicate everything the narcissist owns from your residence**: It may seem surprising, but objects and other items owned by others have a way of keeping you connected. When you continuously come across these objects and perhaps touch them, you tend to remember the person who used to own the item, which in this case, is the narcissist.

  To sever these unseen ties, you will need to gather up all of the things in your home that are owned by the narcissist and send them back through a third party. If you can't do this, you may need to find another way to get rid of them. All that matters is that you don't leave them behind in your home.

- **Release the Memory**: This is also another great way to destroy the connection, but it is a process that will require some time. However, the benefits you stand to gain at the end are well worth it. Think of those events that left you with a lot of trauma that the narcissist was responsible for, then write them in a journal or paper in the form of a letter to the narcissist, expressing all of the pain they caused. Don't hold anything back during this process. If you detest them, now is the time to let it out. However, instead of sending the letter, you can rip it and burn it. It may seem like a strange thing to do, but it is a symbolic act that tends to make one feel better and let go of unhealthy ties.

Also, as you think of the events, do not hold on to them. Instead, feel them and let them go. This is a form of grieving that will allow you to release all that has happened and help you cut down the unhealthy bonds.

Find Yourself Once More

One major effect of narcissistic abuse is that you forget who you are. Instead, you have started to become the narcissist's idea of a perfect person. If this is the case for you, it will be vital to drop the fake person the narcissist has implanted in you. This person is not the real you, and what you feel are not your genuine feelings.

Search yourself for your own needs and desires, as we stated earlier. Try to separate them from the feelings the narcissist has planted into you and try to determine what your specific needs are.

You can also begin this process by doing some things the narcissist always made you believe you couldn't do. Gradually, you will learn that the power lies in you to do whatever you want. With time, you will begin to find that person you are that has been buried deep within as a result of the narcissist.

After you have found yourself, it will be less difficult to determine those things you desire. These desires won't be those that have been implanted by someone else but things that you want. After this, then you can move on to forgiveness.

Find a Way to Forgive

Forgiveness does not have to be the last step, and you are free to forgive the narcissist earlier in the recovery process. However, forgiveness comes here because of its symbolic nature. It is like you are closing this chapter of your life forever and would never open it again.

Holding some resentment and bitterness to someone who betrayed your trust and abused you constantly is normal. However, if you want to complete your healing process, you will have to forgive the narcissist. This will help keep this individual away from your mind permanently.

However, the narcissist is not the only person who requires forgiveness. You will also have to forgive yourself and stop any self-blame. It was not your fault for getting entangled with the narcissist. These toxic people are experienced at what they do and would do anything possible to gain your trust and exploit it. Forgive the narcissist as well as yourself, and your recovery will be complete.

Recovering from Narcissistic Abuse Takes Time

The trauma caused by narcissistic abuse is something that occurred over a long period. It could have been over a period of months or years. This means you will require just as much time to heal from all of the effects and completely recover. Do not blame yourself if it seems your recovery is not as fast as you desire. Healing takes time, and you need to allow yourself all the time you need to mend your heart, mind and soul. The damage is often extensive, and you can't expect a quick fix.

The narcissist spent a great deal of time strategically eradicating your spirit and your individuality. It takes a lot of time to move beyong this. However, this does not mean you can't heal from abuse. The abuse you suffer does not have to determine who you are as an individual. With the right amount of time and commitment, you can free yourself and leave a peaceful and happy life.

Starting Over

Now that you have recovered from the pain and abuse the narcissist put you through, what's next? This is something that has many surviving victims confused. You may believe that getting recovery is the most challenging part of it all; however, knowing what to do after you find your healing can also be a challenging phase.

During the period of the abuse, you probably became used to letting the narcissist make the decisions in the relationship. In fact, you were most likely placing their needs over yours and practically living for the narcissist. So now that you are alone, it is understandable the new situation you have found yourself in is very confusing.

Still, this does not mean you have to be stuck in this phase. Numerous things can give you insights on how you can get a new life once more. This is what we will be having a look at in this section and, hopefully, when you are done with it all, you will know how to go about starting over.

Have Knowledge

The first thing you need to do is to have knowledge. This means educating yourself about the next steps to take in your life. There are a lot of options available to you, which include:

- **Join Support Groups**: Support groups are a valuable and comprehensive information resource. These are groups that offer support for people who have suffered the same things that you did. The great thing about groups is that you have the opportunity to interact with others. You can learn from the experiences of others, and find out how they were able to build a new life after they were done with their healing. It is very easy to find support groups, and a quick Google search will provide you with all the options closest to you. Remember to go with an option that you feel most comfortable with. If your guts say no, then look for an alternative.

- **Attend Therapy**: This is also another great way to get insights. Speaking to a skilled professional can further clear the fog in your mind and place you in the direction you need to be. However, you need to be willing to open up to the therapist or you might not make any headway in your search for clarity. If you don't want to go to therapy by yourself, there is also the option of group therapy. This way, you can listen to the experiences of others, and learn from it while also stating your areas of concern. For some victims, speaking in groups helps them to get the clarity they need faster. Similar to how you find support groups,

running a quick search on Google can show you a list
of top options close to you.

- **Read Online Resource**s: This is an ideal option for
those who want an option that does not need them to
be physically present. If this is the case for you, then
using online resources is the best way to go. There are
online resources available for you, ranging from
seminars to classes, all giving you insights on how best
to approach your new life. In addition to this, you can
leverage the various websites covering this stage of
your life. There is even an allocation for online therapy
and support groups with licensed experts to help you.

The options available to you are limitless, and all you have to
do is pick one that you find most convenient. In the end,
getting the results you desire is what matters.

Believe in Yourself, Your Liberation, Freedom, and Truth

By now, your instincts should be sharper than they once were.
Even though you had learned to ignore them because of the
narcissist who implanted what they desired instead, it does
not mean it is completely gone.

Learn to listen to what it says, and trust that it will lead you
to make the right decision. If you are at a loss as to what to do
next, a great option is to meditate and listen to what your
mind is trying to tell you. Meditation is an excellent option at
this point because it places you on the same wavelength as
your inner-self while pushing out those things that are
irrelevant.

You need to believe in your new-found truth and freedom completely. You are no longer living the illusion created by the narcissist, and it is okay to trust yourself once more. The instant you can do all of these, listening to what your inner person has to say becomes less complicated.

Hang Around People Who Love You

Hanging around people who have a real interest in your life can be another great way to get clarity. They may be willing to push you in the right direction, or you could watch them and see how they live their lives. This could give you ideas on the route you should take.

If you don't have any friends presently, then it is not a problem. You can begin to work toward attracting healthy friends and people who will love you for who you are. To meet new people, you can try classes on topics that interest you or become a volunteer for a cause you are passionate about. However, remember to watch out for the signs of narcissistic behavior. You don't want to bring back another healthy person into your life, considering what you have been through.

Create an Action Plan

Similar to other things in life, having a plan in place can do a lot of good. This plan can serve as a guide that keeps you going when you are at a loss of what to do next. In your action plan include your goals and things you desire to achieve in both the short and long term.

For instance, your action plan could include the following:

- What do I want to achieve in the next five months?
- What new skills do I want to learn?
- How many healthy relationships should I have developed in the coming months?

You can follow the format above to include your action plans. However, the action plan is only useful to you if you can respect it strictly. It is all going to be pointless if you create a plan you don't respect.

Learn New Skills and Get Busy

One of the easiest ways of moving on with your new life is to learn new skills. Since you have already dropped all of the illusions that the narcissist planted in your world, you should have an idea of who you are once more. With the answers you have arrived at, you can learn new skills that appeal to you and use them as a way to stay busy.

There are various relaxation skills that you can learn to provide yourself with clarity like meditation, yoga, and so on. Yoga is great because it has been said to enhance the feeling of mindful awareness in individuals. It is especially beneficial for people who have survived various forms of abuse as it offers you mastery and safety of your body. Easier options include heading to the gym, taking mindful walks or jobs, or just relaxing in the park where you can be one with nature.

Channel your energy to those things that leave you in a peaceful state and learn as you go. Every survivor struggles differently after dealing with abuse and going through the process of recovery. You don't need to follow the exact steps someone who used to be in a similar situation did. Instead, do your own thing and see where it leads.

Conclusion

Congratulations! The fact that you made it here is enough proof that you are tired of being tied down by the abuse from the narcissist. By now, you know that recovery is not easy. It is a process that requires a commitment on your part, and it tends to take a while. However, the benefits you gain are worthwhile.

Still, even with the information available to you, it does not mean you will automatically recover and get your life back on track. You still need to go through the healing process. But the information offered in this book can make this less complicated as long as you can read, understand, and properly implement the strategies I have shared in this book. Healing from narcissistic abuse is an ongoing process, but the truth is that it does get better. Do not forget that you are not to blame, and no one deserves to be abused, including you. You deserve freedom, and you deserve a peaceful and happy life.

I do hope you get the peace you desire with the help of this book. See you with your life under your control once more!

References

10 Signs That You're in a Relationship with a Narcissist. (2019). Retrieved 30 October 2019, from https://www.psychologytoday.com/intl/blog/communication-success/201409/10-signs-youre-in-relationship-narcissist

Smith, M. (2019). Narcissistic Personality Disorder -

HelpGuide.org. Retrieved 30 October 2019, from https://www.helpguide.org/articles/mental-disorders/narcissistic-personality-disorder.htm

Narcissistic personality disorder - Symptoms and causes. Retrieved

30 October 2019, from https://www.mayoclinic.org/diseases-conditions/narcissistic-personality-disorder/symptoms-causes/syc-20366662

There are 3 distinct types of narcissists — here's how to spot

them. (2018). Retrieved 30 October 2019, from https://www.businessinsider.com/how-to-spot-different-types-of-narcissist-2018-1?IR=T

Chan, A. (2018). HuffPost is now a part of Oath. Retrieved 30 October

2019, from https://www.huffpost.com/entry/signs-of-narcissism_n_5a26cf6de4b069df71fa196b

Tracy, N. (2019). Gaslighting Definition, Techniques and Being

Gaslighted | HealthyPlace. Retrieved 30 October 2019, from https://www.healthyplace.com/abuse/emotional-psychological-abuse/gaslighting-definition-techniques-and-being-gaslighted

Gaslighting. Retrieved 30 October 2019, from https://en.wikipedia.org/wiki/Gaslighting

10 Steps to Getting Your Life Back After Narcissistic Abuse.

(2017). Retrieved 30 October 2019, from https://medium.com/@SoulGPS/10-steps-to-getting-your-life-back-after-narcissistic-abuse-96b5c74af29c

The Rollercoaster Of Recovery From Narcissistic Abuse. (2019). Retrieved 30 October 2019, from https://www.aconsciousrethink.com/4032/rollercoaster-recovery-narcissistic-abuse/

Dodgson, L. (2019). The 9 biggest signs you're finally over your

narcissist ex-partner. Retrieved 30 October 2019, from https://www.businessinsider.com/the-biggest-signs-you-are-over-your-narcissist-ex-partner-2018-3?IR=T

Hammond, C. (2019). 12 Survival Tips for Living with a Narcissist

| The Exhausted Woman. Retrieved 30 October 2019, from https://pro.psychcentral.com/exhausted-woman/2017/06/12-survival-tips-for-living-with-a-narcissist/

Fjelstad, M. (2019). 14 Signs You're Dealing With A Narcissist.

Retrieved 30 October 2019, from https://www.mindbodygreen.com/articles/14-signs-of-narcissism